MW00583804

THE MOTOWN SOUND ON WHEELS

ROCKIN' RICHARD HOUSTON

The Motown Sound on Wheels
Copyright © 2018 Rockin' Richard Houston

ISBN: 978-1-5356-1401-6

Dedication

THIS BOOK IS DEDICATED TO all Detroit skaters who were influenced by the Motown Sound. It's dedicated to those skaters at the Arcadia in Detroit, Michigan, where I first learned to skate and where I had my first real job.

It's dedicated to the managers, floor guards, instructors, DJs, friends, buddies, ladies, and men who, throughout the decades, skated with me, put on parties, and inspired me to uniqueness in my skating.

It's dedicated to skaters who have taken Detroit skating, which is the best skating style ever, to other parts of the country.

Introduction

I KNEW THAT THIS SKATING story had to be told! And it was going to take a skater to tell it.

~Rockin' Richard Houston

Contents

Early Life

IT ALL BEGAN AT 419 East Warren in Detroit, Michigan, in 1960. I was nine years old. Our family lived in an apartment building that had eight floors with six apartments on each floor. It was right next door to where the Charles H. Wright Museum of African American History stands now. The back of the building had porches that someone could walk on and see everything that was going on in the back of each apartment. The building also had stairs that went all the way down to the first floor. We played in the back of the building to keep from getting hit by cars in the front. The manager of the apartment building was Mr. Jake Cato. He was the manager, security person, disciplinarian, and maintenance man. If something needed to be fixed, he was the man for the job. If you did something wrong and he caught you, he would get his razor strap and lay it on you. In those days, if a kid did something that he or she shouldn't have done, whoever saw you and knew your mother or father well enough would tear your behind up, call your parents to let them know, and when you got home you would get your butt whipped again. Needless to say, we got into very little trouble.

My father's name was Leroy, but we called him Peanut. He was very well known on the streets of Detroit. He grew up in Black Bottom, which was the east side of Detroit. Often, he would dress me up and take me with him around the city and show me off to his friends. I would ride around in sharp cars that he and his friends would drive. We would hang with guys that were just as clean as we were. He was always sharp and very well dressed. My father did his best to help me learn what life was all about. He was also a father who did whatever he could while he and my mother were together. When they split up, my mother never said bad things about him to me. They were young when they were together. They went through a lot, and in the end, they just could not work things out. My dad passed away a few years ago from bad health. But before he went to meet his maker, we made peace with each other, and I told him that I would make him proud of me.

My mom had to work two jobs to make ends meet, and with me being the oldest, I had to help her out a lot. I had to learn how to cook, clean, and wash clothes at an early age. When she went to work my grandma Pauline and I had to take over. My grandma did not live far from us so sometimes we went over to her house when Mom went to work. She was a good grandma, the type that everyone wanted to have. Whenever my grandmother was needed, she would always be there to help. She would take us to church on Mondays, Wednesdays, and all day on Sunday. It gave my mother time to work extra hours so that she could pay the bills and keep a roof over our heads. She also got the chance to get the rest she needed. There were times when my brothers and I would go over to my aunt Ester's house. She has four boys and that made seven of us: Reggie, Mike, James, Billy, Robert, Ralph, and me. There was always something we could get into around the hood. When all of us would walk the streets, people would think we were a gang. The police would stop us from time to time, but when they found out that we were all related they kept on going. Walking around the hood was something we could do without worrying about gangs. It was hard for me to go out and play with my friends when we were at home because there was always something that needed to be done at home.

I remember, one night, Mom had to go to work and I had to cook dinner for my sisters and brothers. I took out a hen and fried it with some mashed potatoes and corn. That chicken looked so good. I made their plates and went to my room to do my homework. Before I knew it, they came into my room yelling. I thought they were going to tell me how good it was! The next thing I knew, they all jumped on me! I had to fight them all off. They were upset because the chicken I cooked was actually a hen, and no matter how much they tried to separate the meat from the bone it would not part. That was my first bad cooking day. That was a funny memory.

Intro to Roller Skating – My Life's Passion

ONE SATURDAY AFTERNOON IN 1962, Mr. Cato's son, Philip, was going skating and he wanted to take some of us who lived in the building with him to the Arcadia. The Arcadia was on Woodward Avenue near Mack. It was just a few blocks away from the apartment. I did not know then how much my life was going to change from that day on. We went through the front door of the Arcadia and walked up a long walkway to the window to pay for our admission. Philip Cato paid for all of us and gave us a ticket for our rental skates. He took us over to the window to get our skates. My first pair was a size six. I sat down to put them on. When I stood up, I thought I was ten feet tall! Somehow, I made it to the rail, and when I got there, all I could see was this big wooden floor. I thought to myself, "I'll never get around it."

One of the first people I saw was a very tall, big man. With skates on he looked like a giant! As he came closer to the rail where I was standing, he started doing some fancy footwork on his skates. This was the first time I had ever seen someone that big skating indoors, and he was moving on the floor like he was Fred Astaire. The nametag on his shirt said "Buster." I remember my mother telling me that he was the manager of the rink. He moved on those skates with the greatest of ease. His partner came on the floor and they did a few moves together. Watching them, one could tell from their moves that they had been skating a long time together. A slow song was playing, and they did a few moves to it. All of us who'd come with Philip Cato finally got our skates on just as Buster and his

4

partner rolled off the floor. Suddenly, very loud music burst out of the speakers in the rink. The music had a beat that was going through my head and it made me feel like I could skate already. Philip Cato went out on the floor and started skating. I had already been told that he was a very good skater. He really was, too. He went around the floor, building up speed, and then he went the wrong way and slid into the corner. That slide looked as if it took forever. That was the best move I had ever seen anyone do on a pair of skates. He skated to the center of the rink and did some more steps that blew me away. When he got through, he came over to the rail and got me by the hand and took me onto the floor. My eyes were lit up like a Christmas tree. We went around the floor a couple of times with him holding my hand. Every time he would let me go, down I went on my butt. I must have fallen about ten times during one record.

Philip saw my plight and took me over to the smaller rink. That rink had a rail for skaters to hold on to so that they could learn how to get their balance. That worked for a hot second, but the minute I let go of the rail, down I went. So, Philip got me a pair of skates that did not roll so fast, and then he put me back on the small rink. I practiced for months on that small rink, and I must have rolled around that rail a thousand times. But after those months, I was ready to skate on the big floor. I was so excited because I was ready to do my thing! Going onto the main floor was like being in a racecar and getting on a fast track. You had to get right in there really quick. I caught on very fast and was going around with very good balance. But just as soon as I was getting the hang of it and my balance was getting much better, it was time to go home for the day.

Summer vacation came around and the rink was open from 1:00 p.m. to 6:00 p.m. and I went skating every day that I could. The following year, my mother gave me a surprise birthday party at the rink. That was when I got my first new pair of skates. It was like getting a new bike to me. Getting new size-seven skates for my birthday, after wearing rentals for so long, I thought I was **the man**. It took two weeks to break in the new skates, but after that my legs took over. The moves I had been working on were very easy now that I had my own skates. I even had toe stops on the front of my skates. My mind started working on new moves, and then my legs took over. I had been practicing various moves for about a year when, one day, Buster called me into his office. I thought I was in trouble for doing something wrong. He was a very big man, about two hundred and fifty pounds, and messing with him was something you did not want to do. He was the type of person who if someone came into his rink and started something with someone else, he would take both parties into the back room, put boxing gloves on both, and let them go at it until both were out of breath. Then he would make them apologize to each other, and when both of them came out of the back room no one else knew what had happened. Buster was wise that way. He knew that if he could get just the two parties into the back and away from everyone else they would see things differently. Most of the time he was right.

When I got into Buster's office, he told me he had been watching me. He complimented me when he said I was starting to become a very good skater. Then, to my surprise, he wanted to make me a floor guard. The best part was that he was going to pay me for it, too (I would have done it for free). The only other job that I'd ever had was delivering newspapers. This was my first real job, and on skates! As much as I loved skating, it was the best thing that could ever have happened to me, next to getting my skates. A floor guard's duties were to protect people from other skaters when they fell on the floor, help skaters off the floor, and stop skaters from going the wrong way. The floor guard would move people along who were standing along the rail on the skating floor. That would keep the flow on the floor moving. Also, as a floor guard I could stay on the floor and skate by myself when the couples, trios, ladies, and backward couples only were on the floor. And I could get in free and practice all I wanted.

When Buster passed, there were over a thousand people at his home going celebration and we all wanted to say goodbye to him. At his funeral, I saw some of the true skaters that I loved to watch at the rink, guys who had such cool moves that I stole some of them and made them my own. The only way to become a great skater was to watch moves from all the best skaters, and then perfect the moves the way you wanted them.

Skaters Who Influenced Me

SKATING REALLY STARTED TO TAKE shape back in the '40s and '50s at the Forest Club, where Sunny Wilson opened up a rink. This was before Motown hit the airwaves. I have been told that the people who skated back then were a sight to see. After the Forest Club closed down the skaters went to the Arcadia. One of those skaters was a man named Art. He was one of Buster's floor managers. He was a small man, about five foot five, and he could jam on a pair of skates. He could skate in and out and around people as if they were standing still. When I became a floor guard, Art helped me a lot. He had a handgrip that you could not get out of no matter how big you were. No one would mess with me on the skating floor because they knew Art would be right there to help me. I had been looking for him for a long time to see how he was doing. Come to find out, he lived three blocks from my home. I first met his son when I was doing a paint job for a friend of mine. Then he started talking about skating and he said Art's name. As soon as we left the job I went to his home to see him again.

Everyone remembers Nelson, who worked the skate room. He was a big man who limped when he walked, but boy he could skate. That man could work on a pair of skates no matter what was wrong with them. He worked in the skate room with a small white woman named Ms. Skelly. She sold skates to everyone who came to the rink. These two taught me how to fix skates for people. By the time I was twelve years old, I was doing everything in the rink. Still, my passion and all I wanted to do was skate.

My brother Robert (Bobby for short) was the type of brother that you wanted to hang out with. We did everything together. I remember one day we were in the backyard playing tag. I was running behind him when all of a sudden, he jumped the fence, and before I could jump I ran right into the fence and fell over it. Man, I twisted both of my ankles. (I think that's why I can do the drop so well.) Bobby was the one who helped me up the stairs. I could always depend on him being there. It took me four weeks to heal before I could go back to the rink. Those four weeks seemed like a lifetime, and it only made me want to skate even more. I was skating so much that people in our neighborhood barely saw me.

One day I got my brother to go with me, and he had the time of his life. He was not much of a skater then, because he stayed around the house doing some of the things that I used to do. When he did come to the rink he usually just watched a lot and played with the girls. That was his idea of fun.

I also had two close friends, Kenny Mack and Vincent Jones. Kenny was the fisherman of the group. I would get up at 6:00 a.m. and go fishing with Kenny. Before I could put my line in the water good, Kenny would have a bite on his line. Kenny was a great fisherman and he was also a good skater. He did some moves on skates that still make me wonder how he did them. Sadly, in 1986, Kenny passed away. I miss him even now, and whenever I go fishing, all I do is think of my friend. In fact, his sister, Cat, was one of my first girlfriends. Cat would come to the rink just to see me show off in front of her.

Watching my friend Vincent on skates made one think that he was born on them; he was so good. He skated just as sharp as the outfits he wore on the rink. And after all these years of us skating, whenever I see him, he still looks great! Great skating must have run in his family, because his sister Fran was a skater, too. She rode the rails with the best

9

of them. Then, when she skated down the rink going the wrong way, you would have to move or get hit!

Johnny Cato was another friend that loved to hang with us. Johnny Cato was related to Mr. Cato, the apartment maintenance man. No matter where we would go, there he was. Hanging with us, he learned to skate, and got very good at it, too. We all hung together and we all skated together.

Even my brothers and sisters were good skaters. It was a sight to see us on Saturday mornings walking down Woodward Avenue going to the rink. But even though they were good skaters, none of them skated as much as I did. Skating was my life and I skated every chance I got – seven days a week when I could, and sometimes twice a day. I followed that regimen for two entire years. By the time I was fifteen I had become a very good skater.

It was during this same time period that the Motown Sound was getting more and more notoriety with such talented groups as the Four Tops, "Little" Stevie Wonder, the Jackson Five, the Temptations, the Supremes, Smokey Robinson and the Miracles, Junior Walker and the All Stars, Jackie Wilson, and Barry White. Berry Gordy Jr., the man with the vision who was behind the Motown Sound, changed the world with music that was fresh and had a beat that made anyone listening want to dance or, in our case, made us skate like we were on clouds. The Motown Sound gave Detroit an advantage over everyone in the world. We were mastering skating to the sounds of Motown in the '60s, '70s, and '80s.

I had one more year to skate and get it together, because you had to be sixteen to get into skating shows. So, I worked on all of my moves very hard. The more I worked at it, the better I became. Skating became a way of life for me. If I got into trouble at home or out in the streets, my mother knew how to punish me. She would take my skates from me and tell me I couldn't go skating until she said I could. That was a living hell. I even begged her to beat my butt so that my punishment would be over. But she, being a strong woman and a true loving mother, kept to her word of forbidding me to go skating until she said so. She knew that would hurt me more than anything else. My mom was good. Our skates were lined up at the door, and if a pair was missing she would know where that person was.

Just after my sixteenth birthday there was a skating contest at the rink, and I was going to skate in this, my first contest. Even though I was a good skater, on that night I was shaking like a leaf. There were so many people there watching the contest! It was time to do my thing, too, in front of all of them. I did my best and I came in fourth place. Not bad for my first contest, but after that I learned what I needed to do to get first place.

When I entered the next contest, I came in second place and got my first trophy! I was so happy, and my face was just shining. I had the biggest smile, too. It felt like I had come in first. I felt like I was the king of the world. From then on, I skated in as many contests as I could. In fact, I studied the expert skaters, like Duck Chapman, who had Cottrell wheels on high skates. Those wheels made him glide and make half turns as smooth as silk. He would do the grapevine and be working those wheels to his perfection.

"Hairman" was a small man, like me. He got his hair permed next door at Fudge's, a barbershop where some of the best skaters went to get their hair done. You would know when he got his hair permed because he would come into the rink with a white strip around his head. That strip would help when he started to sweat. Hairman thought he was Superman on skates, and some of his moves made you believe it, too. He would get down low and jam some moves that I couldn't even begin to name. All of us spectators kept our eyes on his feet when he was skating, and his skates did the talking.

Another skater, Willie Johnson, was young like I was. We'd get on the rink and try some of the things those expert skaters were doing, but most of the time we landed right on our butts. The guys we were trying to imitate would just look at us and smile and say, "Keep it up, fellas."

Like me, Willie kept practicing skating. And now, years later, when I see him at the rink he is jamming like there is no tomorrow.

Charles Grundy was a jammer, too. He was so good, and he loved skating to the Temptations. So, whenever they played a song by the Temptations, we would just go to the rails and all we could see was Charles rocking those Fo-Macs.

Mike was a very tall skater. He had a long stride to match. In fact, when he slid into the corner you could actually go right through his legs.

Bubba was big and looked as if he was on a football team. Hell, come to think of it, he looked like he *was* the team the way he just skated down the center of the floor. When he did that, everyone else on the floor would part like the Red Sea.

Two other skaters, Boom and Barney, were partners, and they gave Robert, whom I ended up partnering with, and me hell on the floor. They would make up moves that fit their style and jam all night.

Then there was Mo. He was from Flint. Mo was my man. He served overseas at one time. Now he lives in California, working on his magazine and doing very well. He was funny because every time we skated he would watch our every move. Then, when we were not looking, he would try them all. He didn't have to make up any; he just imitated ours.

Arcadia Haywood, may he rest in peace, was the *man* in the rink. His moves were as sweet as sugar and you knew he was going to be a hell of a skater. He loved skating as much as I did. He had the gift of knowing when a person was coming right at him and, at the last second, he would make a sweet turn and would not miss a beat.

Box was one of the skaters that had everyone watching what he did. His skates were not in the best of shape, but boy did he know how to work them. When trios-only skating time came around, Box would take the lead and ride the rail with ten people behind him, slide in the corner with all ten people, and then do it all over again. He would do a move so fast and so smooth that I don't even think he knew what he was doing.

It just came naturally. When I asked him to show me, he would look at me and say, "It will all come to you very soon. Just keep working on it."

Jabow had me follow him one day to help build up my speed. He had those Cottrell wheels on his skates, and I had to use all of my wind to keep up with him. He would cut through the center at the last minute, and I would run right into someone. I could not make that turn as fast as he could.

Green was the "stepper" of the rink. He would get right in the middle of the floor and step to whatever Motown Sound was playing. Whenever we went to Pontiac, MI, there would be an entire group of skaters stepping right with him. Then he would go around the rink and do a jump slide right in the corner and start stepping again.

Frank Bell was the ladies' man. He would come to the rink wearing his sharp clothes. He was over six feet tall, very good-looking, and a damn good skater. He could pick and choose any lady he wanted. I tried to stretch myself to appear to be as tall as he was. I wanted to be like him.

We even had an entire family of skaters with the last name of Rettmen. They were a big family that lived in the projects, and all of them were skaters. They were good for security, too, because if you were cool with them no one would bother you when you went skating. All of them, and I mean all of them, could skate their butts off. I haven't seen them in many years, but a while back, I ran into a few of them and found out that they were gospel singers.

Danny was a floor guard, and a good skater. Don't let the name fool you – Danny was a female floor guard who didn't take any mess from anyone. She had no problem putting you off the floor in a heartbeat, either, if it was necessary.

All of these people were individuals who had skate moves that I just had to learn. I took moves from every one of them and made unique moves of my own from what I got from them. One might think that each of these superb skaters could just instruct me on how to make the moves, but that wasn't so. The moves they created and the ones I conjured up actually came from how the music felt to each of us. How the music made me feel is what enabled me to think up moves and practice them until I was expert at them. That's just the way it was.

Be-Bop Competition

WE HAD SKATING CONTESTS KNOWN as Be-Bops. It was at those Be-Bop contests that I would learn something new from the skaters who were in the contests. As a result, by the time I was seventeen, I had mastered most of the moves that everyone was doing. To help out, the Motown Sound had a groove of its own. That music made your whole body move with an indescribable feeling. It put you in a world of sounds where your mind could just create all kinds of moves on skates!

I would strive to do moves on skates that no one even wanted to try. I was able to do it with the music of the '60s, '70s, and '80s. I was mesmerized by the Motown Sound and the Philly Sound. Then again, who couldn't be inspired to new moves when there were artists such the Spinners, the Stylistics, Delfonics, Jerry Butler, the Manhattans, Wilson Pickett, Deniece Williams, the O'Jays, and Al Green? These were just a few of the artists who influenced my skating career. There were many more. Actually, with that music flowing into my ears, it was easy to make up unique skating moves.

There was a guy named Robert Frett whom I met at the rink. One day we were coming down the center doing the same move and we bumped into each other and ended up doing the same thing when we came to a stop. It was almost creepy as I remember it now. We did the same thing. Well, from that day on we started skating together. Everyone thought we had something special when we skated together because we blended very well. We went to the rink every chance we got. He picked up my moves very fast and I did the same thing with his.

People began telling us that if we continued to skate together we could go into competition and win a lot of skating contests. We took their advice and entered many. Every rink we went to we turned the place out. Robert had a smooth style with good body "English" to help us make up moves. We had one move that we were famous for: we would come down the floor and go into a half turn and come out into a one-leg slide all the way to the corner. People loved to see us execute that move. He and I were one of the best duo teams around. And when songs like "Shotgun," "Rockin' Charlie," "Function at the Junction," "Green Onions," or "Sugar Hips" were playing we turned into one person, not two. We could read each other's vibes and no telling what we would do next. At the end of the record we would look at each other and have a good laugh. That made us the best of friends. The two of us were known all over the city because of the way we skated.

We even went into the Air Force together in 1971 on the buddy plan. When I got off the bus at basic training in Texas, I had my duffel bag and my skates with me. When my drill sergeant saw my skates, he thought I was crazy. The only reason he let me keep them was because there was a skating rink on base. I remember leaving my barracks and going to the skating rink without telling my sergeant. I was turning the rink out when the MPs (military police) came looking for me. My TI (training instructor) had seen that my skates were missing and sent them to the rink looking for me. When the rink owner saw the MPs coming in the door he got on the mike and gave me a heads up. I got my shoes and skated out the back door and back to the barracks. I took my skates off before the MPs could get there. I paid the price, though, because I had to peel over two thousand potatoes. But it was worth it.

Robert and I were kindred spirits. When we had sons, we named them after ourselves. He named his son Robert Jr., and I named my son Richard Jr.

I remember one day it was like rush hour with all the skaters on Telegraph headed to the Rolladium. Jimmy was the manager, and Bobby, Apple, James, and I were some of the floor guards at the Rolladium. The Rolladium rink was bigger than the Arcadia rink, so Robert and I had a lot of room to throw down.

We needed a girl to skate with us so that we could get into contests called trios. We met this girl named Bay-Bay. Man, she was hell on wheels! She was small and smooth and fit right in with the two of us. When we skated as a trio, she was right in sync with us, step by step. We all realized that now we had another way of winning skating contests. I started practicing with her and the more we worked at it the better we became. Bay and I also got into couples only and we became one of the best. We won about five skating contests together.

The Arcadia and Other Skating Rinks

AFTER SKATING WAS OVER AT the Arcadia on Sunday, we would travel to Pontiac, Michigan, to skate at the Rolladium. Their DJ's name at that time was Melvin, may he rest in peace. You had to see this man on wheels. There was no better way to describe him than this: when he came by you, you would picture a jet on wheels! He had us up in Pontiac every week turning the place out. He was a very unique individual. He made all of the clothes that he wore to the rink, and his skates were made from cowboy boots! Every week he wore something different to skate in. He skated at the Arcadia, too; that was why he was so good.

When they had ladies only at the Arcadia, all of us guys, Kenny, Vincent, Robert, Cato, Roscoe, Charley, Jim Danny, Gilbert, Box, Hairman, Haywood, James, and Green, would line up on the rails to watch Pam, Jackie, Poolie, Celestine, Esperanza, the Rettmen girls, Barbara, the Walkers, Angie, Rita, Jenny, Soupy, Kitty, Tanya, and Cookie, among other ladies. And when "Function at the Junction" or "Rockin' Charlie" came on and the DJ announced that it was "Open House," which meant a skater could do whatever he or she wanted to do on the floor, we would encourage them to ride the rails and slide into the corner as fast as they could. It was a sight to see! Motown's music gave Detroit and the surrounding areas their own steps when it came to skating, dancing, and singing. I knew way back then that we had something special to spread around the world.

The music that enabled me and so many other skaters to excel on the rink came from Mr. Berry Gordy's own vision of the Motown Sound, which, together with all of the other music that affected us in the '60s and '70s, I have termed "Movement on Wheels." Some of us skaters were born with a natural rhythm, and when rhythm and music are blended together just right, you pour out your soul on wheels. Because of that "union" between music and my passionate love of skating, I became one of the best on a pair of skates.

Further, I learned during those years that the Motown Sound gave Detroit skaters a reputation like no other in the country. I found out by going to different rinks in different locations and cities that people truly skate differently. Often, we skaters went to different rinks to see if the type of skating we were doing in Detroit was different than what was going on around the country. And yes, it was very different. The Motown Review used to be held at the Arcadia before it got bigger and had to go to a larger place – the Fox Theater on Woodward Avenue in Detroit. Whenever I would go skating in Ohio, it was like going to another planet, and whenever the Ohio skaters saw us skate, they instantly knew that we were ***not*** from Ohio. They paid attention whenever we Detroit skaters got on the floor. Plus, with every move that I made, which was simple to me, they thought it was a hell of a move! So whenever we visited Ohio and skated in their rink, they wanted me to show them how to skate the way we did back in Detroit. What made the task easier was that Motown's music was hitting the area and it was easy to relate to it.

Another skating rink we frequented was the Fairview rink on Mack Avenue. It was on the east side of Detroit. Their rink was located upstairs in the building. Another interesting thing about the Fairview rink was that there were windows upstairs around the rink. So, a skater had to have it together on the floor, because if he or she messed up and made the wrong move, that skater might be going out a window. It was a small rink, so the music was right in the skaters' ears, but that didn't bother us at all because we were jammin' to the sounds of Motown and the '70s sound in general.

The Arena skating rink on Greenfield Road, which was located on the west side, had a very good wooden floor. I mean a skater could slide for what seemed like forever on that floor. The walls of the rink were curved, and you could weave in and out of those curves making up your own moves. It was so fun, and I met a lot of good skaters from the east side there at the Arena. Some of those skaters who went to the Arena also skated at the Arcadia.

Speaking of the Arcadia, there were some parents who wouldn't allow their children to go to that particular rink because it was in a rough area of the city. The Arcadia was located between the Jeffries Freeway on the west side and the Brewster Projects on the east side of Woodward. Skaters found out that at times it wasn't easy to skate at the Arcadia with all the commotion going on. First of all, if you were inexperienced and didn't know what you were doing, you would get run over by other skaters. Then it seemed like every week a fight would break out at that rink. But back in those days, fights were not that bad.

We also went to Belleville, Michigan, to skate. Going to Belleville was like going to the country. A friend of mine, Nate Pittman, went into the corner of the rink too fast. He wound up going right through the back doors, where he landed in a cornfield with cows in it! The speakers in the Belleville rink looked like they were from TV sets. It didn't matter because the Motown Sound came through loud and clear every time. Also, over a period of time, the Belleville skaters learned to jam like Detroit jammers. Not only that, but they didn't have a lot of commotion in Belleville, because the rink was run by the chief of police. So, if a skater started something, off to jail he or she went. It took us about thirty minutes to get to the rink, and it was well worth the ride.

The rink in Southwest Detroit was called the Rollercade. It was like a matchbox inside. The owners of the rink were the Folks family. Earl Folks was the DJ and the manager. When he turned those speakers on you could almost see the bass bounce off the walls because the rink was so small! We learned to put our skates on real fast there because when you sat down to put them on, you were already on the floor! That little rink was marble, and it was very smooth. In fact, whenever Earl would put on a Motown jam we rolled around so fast one would think a tornado was in the place! No matter how smooth that floor was, when the music came on its sound would take over your body and not let it go until the record was over. That feeling would come over me whenever I'd hear a record like "My Girl" by the Temptations or "What's Going On" by Marvin Gaye. A person had to be a good skater like the ones I hung with: JR, Richie Rich, Deborah, Derrick Bell, QZ, Leroy, Doug, Wanda, George, and Carl Green. When the Motown Sounds were played, even Earl Folks, the DJ, came out of the record booth and got on the floor.

The Carousel was another rink in Southwest Detroit, where we skated. It was actually down the street from the Rollercade. The Carousel was small like the Rollercade, except that it had a wooden floor that let us slide with our Fo-Mac wheels. Fo-Mac wheels on skates allowed us to do a lot of different things on the floor. A skater could slide and grip the floor with those wheels, unlike a soft wheel that grips the floor all the time. Not only that, but Detroiters bought more Fo-Mac wheels than any other city in the world. In many other states, skaters wore softer wheels that gripped the floor to give them speed. And after wearing them for so many years, they found themselves locked into them. When those skaters would put on a pair of Fo-Mac wheels and skate, they'd slip every time they turned the corner on the floor.

Our group also went to rinks in Flint, Michigan, and in Mt. Morris. Both of these rinks had good wood floors and very good sound systems. It didn't matter where the rink was located. If there was a good floor to skate on and good music to skate to, Detroit skaters would be there. The skaters in Flint loved to skate and they caught on quickly. Their style was like ours; plus, they always gave great skating parties. It was easy to see that the skating clubs in Flint took skating very seriously, just like we did, and would travel any place to get down on some wheels. On Wednesdays we would skate until 1:30 a.m. At the end of the night the rink would have open house. Open house was when skaters could go around the floor as fast as they could and slide into the corner. Truthfully, a person could smell the wheels burning from the long slides. It was an amazing sight that had to be seen to understand why we did it. The sound system at the Flint rink was really good and it just made us jam even harder. If a person skated just one time at that Flint rink, he was hooked.

Detroit Roller Wheels on Schoolcraft was a big rink and the wood floor was very good to skate on. We had a lot of fun there and gave lots of skating parties. We also put on skating shows for the kids, had skating contests, and more. You name it and we did it at Detroit Roller Wheels. Elton, the manager, worked very hard to keep the skaters in line. He also put on skating shows with the kids and taught lots of people to skate. The owners of Detroit Roller Wheels were very easy to work with and they extended themselves to help make skating parties successful. They are very high on my list of people who believed in what we were trying to do. I gave two jazz skating parties there and they took very good care of me. They also owned Northland skating rink. Northland was a hot place to skate. One of the best in the country, in my opinion. It had a very big wood floor where a skater could really show off all of his or her skills. If someone wanted to put on a big party, Northland was the place to go. Elton, who was my good friend, also managed the Northland rink. He would also help us get good deals when we wanted to rent the rink or put on shows.

Whenever we wanted to leave the country to go skating, Canada was where we went. Going skating in Canada was like going back in time! They seemed to be stuck in the 1970s. We would hear a Motown record every now and then. We had to start bringing some of our own records for them to play. When the Canadian skaters would come over here to learn our moves, they would go back to Canada and show off in front of their friends. Their rink was new and over time, skating there, we began to see more and more people of color skating at that rink, getting down to the Motown Sound with us. The Motown Sound works on anyone, no matter what color they are. When that sound hits your body, you are hooked for life.

There was a rink in Inkster, Michigan, called the Safari. We all used to skate there from twelve midnight to four in the morning. The Safari had a very big wooden floor, and it also had a stage for us to put on skating shows. Whenever we had cabaret skating parties we could bring whatever we wanted to drink. It wasn't a good idea to skate after a few drinks. Five hundred people looked like a thousand after a few drinks, because you would see double. But we had some very good times there. Great skaters like "Nate the Skate" would go to the Safari to throw down on Friday nights, and if a person wanted to learn some new moves from some of the best skaters, the Safari was one of the places to go.

On the east side of Detroit, off Conner and Warren, was the Arcade. In the beginning it was a bowling alley. Sometime later it was turned into a skating rink. It was small with a wood floor and a hell of a sound system. That sound system at the Arcade made the Motown Sound jump out at you. We would leave that rink with dust all over our faces from the skating floor!

Skateland rink was also on the east side. It was a medium-sized rink with lights all around the floor. On that wood floor a skater could slide very smoothly. On Sunday nights we would have a session from 9:00 p.m. to 1:00 a.m. – twenty-five and over. Anyone attending that Sunday-night session would have to park two blocks away unless they got there early. And there was no doubt that it was going to be a good time when Little Ken, Big Ken, or Earl the Pearl started the music. On Sunday night, Skateland was the place to be. It made a skater feel like he or she was back at the Arcadia because Skateland was reminiscent of the Arcadia.

On Saturdays at Skateland, sometimes there were more than two thousand kids in line to get down on their skates. By the way, my son

Greg got his first job as a floor guard there, and he started skating very well, too. Watching him as a floor guard and skating made me see myself growing up all over again. Detroit is a great place to learn how to skate. In my opinion, Detroit is the skating capital of the world. Our style is so unique from the rest of the world, and it's all due to the music of the '60s, '70s, and '80s and the Motown and Philly Sounds.

Skatin' on Fo-Mac Wheels

WHEN THE WEST COAST STARTED skating to the Motown Sound, they did not know a thing about Fo-Mac wheels, unless they came from Detroit. Many people out West wouldn't buy Fo-Mac wheels because wearing them outdoors would mess up the wheels. Detroit skaters were good on Fo-Mac wheels because of years of wearing them indoors. Skating was more of a winter sport for us; the fall and winter seasons were the perfect times for my buddies and me to skate. We did skate during the warmer months, but when it was cold outside and there were four or five inches of snow, we'd all head to the skating rink and skate for a few hours.

We also used something else that others around the country didn't use – toe stops. Toe stops are very close to the floor on the front of the skates. They enable the skater to take off very fast and allow the skater to spin very fast on the wheels. When I would go out of town most of the people I saw skating were wearing plugs in their skates. Plugs make skaters have to bend their ankles much more to the ground and take off moving from side to side, and when spinning, skaters have to use all the wheels on their skates. Detroit skaters tie their boot strings all the way up, too, which gives added strength to their ankles. It is easily possible to sprain or even break an ankle when bending more than is necessary. Detroit skaters like to get strength from their whole leg, enabling them to do different tricks and slides. Not only that, but we skate on a one-two type of beat, and skaters from other cities skate on a three-four type of beat. There's nothing wrong with that; it's just another difference between Detroit skaters and other skaters.

But no matter what kind of skates they wore or how they tied them up or how low the toe stops were, the Motown Sound just made all of them do different things. The sounds of Motown made skaters make up their own moves. If there were millions of people skating at the same time, the Motown Sound would permeate all of their bodies and make them create their own style. The sounds of Motown were magical. My friends and I loved skating so much that we could go skating at one rink for four hours, leave that rink, and go to another rink that same day. Yeah, we were hooked on roller skating.

After a time, I started seeing more and more out-of-town skaters with Fo-Mac wheels. That told me that they liked what they saw us Detroit skaters doing on our Fo-Mac wheels and wanted to learn something new. I even bought some soft wheels to learn some of their moves. It was a good strategy and learning experience for me, too. Putting on different wheels changed or added moves that I could perform on the floor.

The Gong Show

IT WAS WHEN THE ARCADIA closed down that I had a change in life. I knew that I had to go out into the world to see for myself just how our style, the Detroit style, of skating was different. It was that event of the Arcadia closing and the determination and passion that I had for skating that got me on *The Gong Show*. I called Los Angeles, CA, where *The Gong Show*, hosted by Chuck Barris, was filmed. I wanted to get a date to perform on *The Gong Show*. I was so very excited when they gave me a date to come to Los Angeles. I got on a Greyhound bus in downtown Detroit and three days later I was in Los Angeles.

The process was longer than expected but it didn't deter me at all. After I passed the audition test I had a two-week wait before I would be on the show. I had determined that I was not going back to Detroit until I got on *The Gong Show*, so I stayed in a hotel until show time. It was well worth the wait. I even had some of my friends from Detroit come visit and help me pass the time. One friend, Mike, the only bass guitar player I know with three fingers, took me to NBC Studios. I stayed with Mike and his family when it was time to get down. They made me feel just like I **was** part of their family. And just like family, they put the pressure on me. They told me that if I did not win I would have to get my own ride back to their house. But I had to win – not just for me, but for Detroit, my family, and my friends, too.

Walking into NBC Studios to do *The Gong Show* that day gave me a feeling I just can't explain even now. It was like I was in another world. I arrived at 9:00 a.m. and found out that there were ten shows to be taped that day. I was led to a room where other performers were waiting, and I was told to stay there until my name was called. The staff assured me that I would be in one of the shows. So, I waited; it was a long time, but I waited anyway. While I waited, I saw so many stars come and go; it took my breath away. The only disappointing thing was that we were not allowed to have cameras and take pictures. I could have filled an entire photo album up if I could have taken pictures, though.

After I waited for five hours my name was called and I was told that I would be on the next show and to get ready. Of course, the butterflies were doing their thing in my stomach. My turn to perform came and I had to beat a score of 29 out of 30 points. They ushered me to my place on the stage; the record I chose to skate to was "Feet Don't Fail Me Now." The curtain opened up and for a total of five seconds I was in shock. After that I was unstoppable. I skated my butt off and when my performance time was over, I waited to see what scores the judges would give me. Arte Johnson gave me 10 points! Jaye P. Morgan gave me 10 points! Allen Ludden gave me 10 points! I earned 30 points, which was enough to win the show. The feeling of joy I had when I won was indescribable.

But that wasn't the last of *The Gong Show* for me. Three months later, they called me back to be a guest on the show. They flew me there and put me up in a hotel with access to a limousine! They paid me and treated me like a star. They even put me in the union, so I could get checks every time my particular shows were aired on television.

Motown Skaters are What's Going On

AFTER *THE GONG SHOW*, I knew Motown skaters had something big going on. I would talk to former Detroit skaters who had moved to other cities and they just confirmed what I knew already – us Motown skaters had a style all our own.

An excellent skater from Detroit and a good friend of mine, Miguel Norwood, had been living in Los Angeles for more than twenty years. He was also into films. While I was in Los Angeles, he took me to various clubs where I met a lot of stars. Miguel confessed that he turned those L.A. rinks out because of the Motown style he learned in Detroit. When Motown moved to Los Angeles, migrating Detroiters took the Motown style of skating with them, and everyone knew the difference in styles.

Gloria Taylor (Glo-Glo) was another skater from Detroit. She helped me a lot whenever I visited L.A. She lived to skate and knew where all the rinks were. All Glo-Glo had to hear was "Let's go skating," and she'd beat you to the car. She moved to L.A. and has taught there for more than twenty years. She met and knows all the stars that roller skate. For a time, she even had me doing TV shows like *ABC Afterschool Special*. She was also very instrumental in putting together Detroit skating parties in Los Angeles. To date, she and Marilyn Coleman (Socks), another Detroit jammer who moved to L.A., still put on a Detroit skating party in Los Angles once a year. These two women, along with my friend Marcus Milton, have kept the Detroit skating style alive in Los Angeles, California.

Bill Butler, My Inspiration

OFTEN PEOPLE ASK ME WHO the one person is that I admire the most on a pair of skates. My answer is always Bill Butler. Bill was one of the first skaters who went out of town and made a name for himself. He started here in Detroit at the Arcadia, just like so many of us did. Then he caught the skating bug. He was confident in himself that he had a special talent for skating, and he went to New York to prove it. He turned the place out!

Bill Butler also wrote a book entitled *Jammin'*. It was the first book about our type of skating. He was also my inspiration to go and perform on *The Gong Show*. Meeting him was on my bucket list. So, I went to New York and went straight to a rink where he skated. When I got there, I found out that the rink was inside a tall building with eight floors. I went around the block three times before I found the place. At first, I thought someone had lied to me about where the place was. But as I started up the stairs toward the rink, I heard music. I ascended higher and higher up those stairs; I was so excited. When I got to the top floor and went through the door, I couldn't believe my eyes. People were skating everywhere, and the music was bouncing off the walls! All I could say was, "Thank you, Lord! I'm in skate heaven now."

When I got over my initial shock and excitement, I sat down someplace and started to put on my skates. Seated right next to me was Cher! I had to pinch myself to make sure it was real. I spoke, and she told me that she couldn't wait to get on the floor and turn it out. I was still in a daze to think that Cher was talking to me! I told her that I'd come all the way from Detroit to skate. Then she smiled and said, "See you on the skating floor."

When I put my things up I went over to the rail to see what the floor looked like. Everyone was standing around someone in the middle of the floor and they were making a lot of noise because of what he was doing on his skates. I went out to get a better look and there was someone doing some mean skating moves that reminded me of our style back home. When the record was over everyone was all over him. It was Bill Butler, my inspiration. When I got the chance to talk to him, I told him I'd come from Detroit to meet him and to see his style. He was very glad to meet me. After a few records of watching me skate, Bill came over to me and told me that I was a "damn good skater." Then he asked if I would skate with him and Cher on trios. I was only too excited and honored to skate with both of them. In a few words, we turned the place out! Skaters were coming up to me asking me if I was Bill's brother. Wow, what a compliment that was.

I got off the floor after that and watched Bill jam. All I could say was "He is one mean cat on wheels." The first thing they asked me was if I was from Detroit. Then Bill and I skated during men only. Again, the two of us lit the place up. That's a night I will never forget.

Skating gave me the great opportunity and privilege to meet many famous people who also loved skating. Jim Brown, who even came to Flint, Michigan, to skate, Fred Williamson, Bernie Casey, Kareem Abdul-Jabbar, and John Amos were all famous stars I met who loved to skate. I even skated in a contest at Marla Gibbs's club in L.A., and I won second place. Ms. Gibbs told me to stay with it and that good things would come my way. I believe that, too.

It's wonderful to see skaters spreading their wings and going to other cities just to find out what I've said all along. Detroit skaters get on the floor and their style of skating is different. It's Motown. For instance, Cynthia Travis is a lady who is so smooth on skates you have to constantly keep an eye on her, because if you blink, you'll miss some damn good moves. One of her best moves is when she goes into a fake half turn reverse inside slide with a left kick (what a move) – it is unbelievable. Skating hasn't done her any harm either. She has been skating many years and still looks like she's in her twenties. One day I will host a skating TV show that will be as hot as *Soul Train*. It will be a show to let people who don't skate better understand what I've been trying to say in this book. They will know what I mean when I talk about the Motown Sound on wheels.

My Passion…My Dream

THERE ARE SO MANY OTHER skaters who moved out of Detroit and went to other cities in the country and took center stage when they put the Motown style on any skating floor. There are lots of people who truly believe that our style is the best. I want to go on record saying that our style is DIFFERENT from the rest.

Along with other skaters, we had a show here in Detroit called *Rolling Funk* on local Channel 62 in the late 1970s. The mastermind behind this TV show was Leonard Johnson, who was a great skater, too. Leonard and a few of us jammed for a short time on television, but it did not go over big, because the time just wasn't right then and many of the skaters were still working on their own unique style.

Again, in the early '90s, Mr. Davis of Northland skating rink had a TV show called *Soul on Wheels*. Sadly, the sponsors ran out of money and could not keep it up.

Because of my love for skating, when I put my skating TV show together, it will have more than enough sponsors to keep it going. It's going to take a lifelong, passionate skater like me to get it right. When I do get my television show, people from all over the world will be coming to Detroit to see some of the best roller skating in the world. Many of us skaters delight in helping each other out. We help any way we can when it comes to giving a skating party at a rink. We take skating to the next level, a level few skaters have ever gone to.

Rockin' Richard Houston

Our love for skating takes us all over the country. We travel from state to state just to strap on a pair of skates. To put it in perspective, here in Detroit, we take skating just as seriously as the Chinese take martial arts in their country. When a Michigan skater with cool moves performs in another state, there is no doubt that he or she will stand out in a crowd, all because the skater's style will be different from that of the rest of the skaters. It's that way because of the music we grew up with – the Motown Sound and all the soul music we had that permeated a skater's entire body and even his soul. That sound took you over, giving you a vibe to work with. That's why skaters from Detroit and the surrounding area were good at skating, for sure, but they were also good at singing and dancing! That sound that started a movement so long ago is still around today, and I have no doubt that it will still be around in the decades to come. It's truly amazing, because now that I am older, and after all those years of skating, I *still* can't tell you in words how good it feels. You have to find it out for yourself.

I may not have mentioned your name in this book, but you can always let me know by email who you are and what your style is. You can tell me what Motown music gets all inside of you and causes you to invent moves that are uniquely you. You can send me a video of you on the roller rink skating to the music of Motown that fills you with smooth moves and more. If I can, I want to get every story I can about how the Motown Sound made you better on wheels *and* in life.

Until that time, I'm ROCKIN RICHARD HOUSTON, and I'm skating my way through life.

Rockin' Richard Houston
Email: Flomat777@aol.com

Rockin' Richard Houston's Acknowledgements

- ♫ Kevin and Lori – keeping the Motown style alive and holding things down in California. They have a web page that's also on the mark about what's going on in the skating world. Keep up the good work.

- ♫ Ira Hestler (may he rest in peace) worked on most of the skaters' cars to help them get to all the rinks. You should have seen him hit the corner; you could almost smell the wheels when he slid. You could just ask him to do a jump slide in the corner and watch his face light up.

- ♫ What's up, KC? Time to lace up and jam again. You know your stuff.

- ♫ Bernice Reed, between skating and fishing, I think we got you hooked on skating. You make that half turn look so easy.

- ♫ Gwen, you have come a long way. All that work practicing your moves and look at you now. You became a true jammer in a very short time.

- ♫ Charles Haywood was one of my favorites. I taught him some things and he just ran with them. His style was very close to my own. He had a mind that could make up moves as fast as his feet could move. He passed away a few years ago and we will never forget his love for skating.

- ♫ Joi Skathon is the Queen of the South, and she is spreading the Motown style in the Atlanta area. Every year when she gives a skating party it's a hit. In fact, I've been to some of her parties that were jammin' with over a thousand other skaters working the wood. After your more than sixteen years of jammin', my hat goes off to you. We wish you the best.

♪ Lorna Hubbard will make you keep both eyes on her style. Just call her Ms. Glide. Her daughter Justina can work the floor, too.

♪ When I skate with Calvin Fant I think about Robert Frett. He has a very good stride in all his moves. He works as a floor guard in Northland. I would put him in my skating movie any day.

♪ Wiggles, whenever you skate, everyone watches you with both eyes wide open. The way you move on those wheels – not to mention when you knock down those pins at the bowling alley – you think you're sliding into the corner. Keep bowling 300. You are able to get people to skate using very few words. Calvin is one of those people.

♪ Chucky makes it look so easy you would think he was born on skates. I have seen him do some moves that made me want to ask him, "How did you do that?" But I knew he would echo what I have told people who ask me that same question – it was a "feeling" move that happened at just that moment.

♪ Jerome (Motorcycle Man), keep on working on those moves. They will come together very soon.

♪ Jammin' Reggie is going to give the skating world a lot of good shows. He can keep you watching his moves, because his style is smooth and his skating with costumes is very entertaining to see. The kids love to see him as Snoopy on skates.

♪ Little Rick Anter impresses a lot of people with his fast, and I mean fast, fresh moves. Keep an eye on him if you can.

♪ El Williams (Mr. Glide) can slide from one side of the floor to the other.

♪ Norman and his wife, Joanne, will travel from coast to coast with their ice-skating-on-wheels style. All you have to say is "Let's go rolling." Joanne, I hope your health gets better.

♪ Star is the only female DJ at Detroit Roller Wheels who can play music and skate up a storm at the same time.

♪ Noah will give a skating party every month; that's how much he loves skating. Now anyone can pick up his CD of great music.

♪ Bauship and his brother Kenny Mike will do flips and jumps that will just rock a crowd to the point that all they want is more.

♪ Jessie, you're getting better, and faster than you think. Soon you will master all those steps. Good skaters will always see the difference when a person is improving their skating skills.

♪ Diane, no matter how much you fall, remember, just keep at it. Everyone falls from time to time, no matter how good they are. The only way to learn how to get to the top is to keep working on your moves.

♪ Ronald and James Dockery have a collection of different moves. Just when I thought they were running out of moves, they would come to the rink and make up more.

♪ Thomas (The Hitman) Hearns can do more than just box. We all know one of the reasons he has strong legs is because of the skating he did when he came to Northland skating rink to keep his legs in shape. He would skate trios with us, and then thank us for the workout.

♪ Doc Thomas, Hearns's bodyguard, can ride his police bike like he is coming down the rails to slide in the corner. Just move out of his way.

♪ Lisa, you know I can't talk about Flint without talking about you. We all know you're one of the top female skaters in Flint, and you have good moves that match your good looks.

♪ Earl "The Pearl" can rock the house at the DJ booth and he can roll on the floor to the Motown Sound.

♪ When they are not in the DJ booth, expect to find Little Ken and Tall Ken turning the sounds and skating up a storm on the floor.

♪ When a DJ is on, we will sweat all night long. If it weren't for the jamming DJs all over the country, we would not be as big as we are today. So, my hat goes off to all of you guys that keep us ROLLING.

♪ Big Bob is an out-of-state DJ from New York who turns the sounds at a lot of the out-of-state parties. He's not a skater but he kicks out the jams as if he were. Keep up the good work, Mr. DJ of the Year.

♪ Robert the DJ can play some mean sounds when we are in Northland or Canton.

♪ DJ Spinradio Seabrooks can be heard on the radio putting out skating jams every week, and his wife, Kylah, is one of our Motown jammers too. She loves to hit a good slide in the corner.

♪ The only thing I will say about Little Bit is that in the short time you've been skating, you have learned more than some people have learned in a lifetime.

♪ Pops, you have been through a lot with your health, and all you want to do is go skating. Keep it up and get better soon.

♪ You had to have been from the Big D to understand what I'm saying about these skaters.

♪ If only Nippy were back on skates to show us some of those out-of-sight moves.

♪ If you want to see a fashion show on wheels, watch Dee, Annette, Shirelle, and Dora; they can jam on skates and look good doing it.

♪ Earnest can jam on his wheels just as good as riding on his bike. Teach me to ride like you.

♪ Jimmy is a skater that you never know what will happen with. Once, Jimmy and I were headed right at each other. But before I could move, he got around me and was on his way down the floor.

♪ Brother Khalifah Rahman moves so fast on a pair of skates all I can say is "Now you see him and now you don't."

♪ Dennis Johnson, known as Spanky, is Mr. Cool on skates; he never breaks a stride.

♪ Mabel Madison grew up going to the Arcadia. Just call her Ms. Motown; you can see it every time she skates.

♫ Roosevelt Richardson and his main man Robert can hang in there with the best of them. When it's time to jam, let them have the floor and they will keep you looking.

♫ Terri Samuel can glide without even missing a beat on the floor; just try keeping up if you can hang.

♫ James Jones can spin circles around you before you even catch on; he will make you dizzy keeping your eyes on him.

♫ When I think about a bus driver, Jerry's name comes to mind. Good thing he can skate as well as he does, because the girls that skate with him need to wear a parachute! Talk about being airborne.

♫ Little Dave can jam in and out of people like they are standing still. Being small helps a lot, right Dave?

♫ Monique Whitley, with her hourglass frame, will make you watch more than the smooth stride she has.

♫ Keith K. Wilson, known as "Rock," does just that – rock all over the place no matter what rink he's in.

♫ Bobby, Skateland's manager, throws down when we can get him on the floor. He's small and fast as hell.

♫ Lavell is another of Skateland's managers. One day, Lavell, we will get you to dust off those skates and get you on the floor, so you can do your thang.

♫ If you want to see a white boy jammin' on Sunday night at Skateland, watch Snow Cone, Detroit's own comedian.

♫ Darius will be close behind him, working the floor.

♫ Al, known as Lefty, it must be magic the way you keep on improving your skating skills. Keep up the good jammin'.

♫ To Judy, my skating partner at Northland, skating with a jammer like you makes it easy for me to look good. You still skate like a bird in flight (sweet).

♫ Sam Brogdon, you were starting to get down with the best of us until your partner, Norman, passed. He will always be in our hearts for the things that he loved to do on skates.

♩ Deborah Conner, you're one of those Flint angels who must have been born on skates too. Your style is like poetry in motion.

Skating has brought a lot of couples together, and their love for skating has kept them in tune with each other.

♩ Red and Baby Jim have been skating together more years than I can count. Red is sixty-five and still slides into the corner.

♩ Crystal and Butch met at the rink and got married; I drove the limo and taped their reception. They are still jamming today.

♩ Keith and Deborah Harbin have been going skating together for so long. In fact, I think that's the only way they will come to the rink. They also skate very well together.

♩ Elvin (Buff) Roper and Alice Alexander have skated together for a long time. I have seen them in contests, too. They are skating just that well and performing moves that will blow your mind.

♩ When Wilson and Theresa Robertson come skating, they are the envy of the rink. The clothes they wear are very much the same, and after all these years of skating they have a style all their own.

♩ Abdul Raheem makes skating shirts for the skaters. He and his wife go all the way back to the start of jammin' at the Arcadia.

Acknowledgements Continued

♪ When Edward (Slim) Freeman takes the floor, his moves are still outstanding to see.

♪ Rhonda Scott is smooth, and her ladylike moves remind you of a model coming down a runway stride for stride.

♪ James Johnson skates at the Rollercade. He's tall and very swift on his feet. You should see his mean half turn.

♪ Rain, sleet, or snow can't keep Curtis Evans from going skating. That is how much he loves to roll at the rinks.

♪ Linda Brown will reveal all of her skating talents if you put the right Motown record on.

♪ Ron Jackson even showed me a move that I still use today. I'm almost as good as when he does it.

♪ Annette Page, you have improved so much with your skating. Now, **all** the men want to skate with you.

♪ When it comes to balance, I think of John Meeks and Albert D. Young. You guys must have wings on your feet.

♪ Lucky, your words of encouragement make me feel very gifted to know you. I'm very proud to be your friend.

♪ When I think of speed, Yvonne's name pops up. When we skate together, we move so fast that if there were a skating cop on the floor, we would get pulled over and get a skating ticket.

♫ To Michelle, Miss Skate USA, you're the one who works on everyone's hair to make them look like a million dollars when they get to the rink. Stay as fine as you are and take care of yourself overseas.

♫ With a drop of a hat, Lester Johnson will go from state to state to get down on some wheels. Glad to know you.

♫ Not only does Stephanie Wade look good, she can also take charge on the skate floor with her "skills on wheels." Just watch her hit that corner and break into a long slide.

♫ If you want to see someone zip around the floor like he's in a racecar, watch Jake Norman's moves.

♫ Don't misjudge Ted Burrell; he can move through a crowd and never touch a soul.

♫ When Cora Elliott gets motivated on wheels, you have to drag her off the floor – if you can catch her.

♫ I have seen Robert Jones stop on a dime and pick up the change.

♫ How can you not notice Aleeca D. Woods on the floor? She can overtake you in a hot minute with that style of hers.

♫ My good friend Bone loves to do my drop, and he does it very well. Keep those legs in shape.

♫ Harold D. Luke and Norman Glover are Brewster Project jammers who can put a Motown record to shame with their style. Check them out on "Shotgun."

♫ Edward Colbert has a style that everyone loves. When he gets into his groove, he can leave a chill down your back.

♫ If you give a skating party and want to hear some of the sounds from back in the '60s and '70s, call Larry. He has everything from "Shotgun" to "Rockin' Charlie."

♫ Tall Tony's feet might hurt, but you would never know it when that Motown Sound starts going through his body. He will go and sit down for a while until his feet feel better and then hit the floor again.

♫ Big Hank can ride the rails at will. So, you should move out of the way or you could get run over.

♪ Jackie Franklin is as smooth as glass on skates. When she hits one of those slides, she just goes on and on.

♪ Shelly Smith just needs a beat to start her motor, then off she goes, throwing down. She will keep it up until the music stops.

♪ I put some Fo-Mac wheels on Donna's skates, and now she thinks she is Rockin' Richard with her new moves.

♪ Theresa Washington is one of my Arcadia fans. She is a very good artistic skater with style.

♪ Pee Wee can do a split in a trio and never miss a beat.

♪ Big Willie thinks he was born on skates. I think his first pair of shoes had wheels on them!

♪ Carlton Smith will surprise you with his skills on wheels. He hit one move that I still can't do. Keep an eye on him.

♪ Dana (Dan) Davis can wear out a pair of skates with that smooth style of his. He hit a slide and I could smell the wheels burning from it.

♪ Deborah Martin has the spins of an ice skater. When she goes into a spin, you forget she is on roller skates. You should see her and Tony Rome jam together. I would just sit down and watch them all day long, because I know they will put on a show that should be seen by everyone.

♪ Brenda – Soupy is what I call her – is one of the skaters that lived in the same building that I lived in when I grew up on Warren Avenue in Detroit. Now she has the looks and style to match all the graceful moves she executes.

♪ Soupy's husband, Robert (Peanut), is a damn good skater who skated with us back in the '70s. He's a very good friend who will give you the shirt off his back.

♪ Regina is Ms. Ballerina. Ice skaters even learn from her. She was able to take that Motown beat and put artistic moves with it, and the results are amazing to see.

♪ Peaches, it only took you a short time to become a jammer, and now you're in our trios hanging with us like you never missed a beat.

♪ Byron, I know you have been jammin' for a long time now. As good as you are, it's easy to see why all the ladies want to skate with you.

♪ When you see Big James coming down the center with his two-hundred-eighty-pound frame about ready to slide into the corner, get out of his way, because he will be moving like he is in his big rig! When I skate with him and we go into a turnaround high hop, it takes some time for me to come back down to the floor.

♪ Very few big people can be swift and smooth and make the wheels do whatever they want them to do like Big Ron (may he rest in peace). He always gave a holler when he was on his way down the floor to hit a corner.

♪ Big Bill and Big Reggie would come down to hit a corner, and if they had to, they would take you with them if you got in their way. Don't get me wrong, they were not out for blood; that was just their way of jammin.' If you knew how Detroit skaters jammed, you would get out of the way fast.

♪ Joe – we call him the picture man because he takes a lot of the pictures at most of the skating parties. You can't miss him; he loves to wear shorts.

♪ Nate Pittman was one of the St. Stephens skaters. That rink was in a church basement in Detroit. He's like a rubber band that can bend in ten different directions, and he can skate circles around everyone. I got put out of a rink in Ohio because the owner thought I was Nate. Nate loves to slide into the corner leaning all the way back.

♪ The Walkers are a family of skaters that have been around as long as I have. We all look so much alike that everyone thought we were brothers and sisters.

♪ My good friend Yancy, who is jammin' in heaven, was a leader when it came to skating. He believed in teaching the art of skating. I gave a skating party, and he put on a show with four chairs and four ladies. It's a show that we will never forget.

♪ Every Martin Luther King Jr. Day we will be thinking about Charles the fireman who passed, and Norman the police officer who was cut down in the line of duty. They were skaters, too, and I had great times teaching them a lot of my moves.

🛼 I remember when Cortez could only do a few moves. He worked hard at it and now he's at the top of his skating game.

Watching Detroit skaters will help you learn to jam.

🛼 Vernon Harris and Haywood can put some of that Arcadia soul in your blood when you see them get down as a skating couple.

🛼 When Richard W. Manning, known as the Bird, starts sliding, you wonder if he will ever stop.

🛼 Jeff the painter is learning how to produce some mean moves on the floor. Keep it up and I'm going to have you skate with me hitting some slides.

🛼 Kathy Stanley will give you that St. Stephen's style all night long.

🛼 William Waddell is from the old school and can still rock the house. He keeps telling me that he is retired, but skating is like a drug that you can't get enough of.

🛼 Pat Byrd is a skater who put together a club called Detroit Connection that puts on big shows every year.

Skaters come from all over the country for a weekend of skating and dancing.

🛼 Bonnie Gibson loves skating so much that she drove from Detroit to Atlanta by herself just to skate at a skating party. Now that's a true skater.

🛼 Denise Hamilton is one of my skating partners, and we blend together as one. She can rock the house in a heartbeat.

🛼 Josie, who is in her seventies, doesn't look a day over fifty. She can still do a split on skates. She was also Ms. Senior America in the late '90s, and she performed on skates.

Michigan has a lot of skating clubs because we started skating to that Motown sound FIRST.

♪ The Detroit Rockin' Rollers are a group of skaters who will put on a show the world will soon see. They have some skaters that are on the right road to be great someday very soon.

♪ Another club called Five Star is made up of a group of ladies who will keep you amazed with their sexy style of skating. Their hot moves and sexy outfits will keep you watching.

♪ The Microstars, a group of skaters that I'm a part of, can skate on top of tables if we have to, all with tuxedos on. When you see us perform, watch out – we are breathtaking.

♪ Detroit Connection Now, my girl Vanessa Jones

♪ Detroit Screamin' Wheels, Elijah Hayes

♪ Divas on Wheels, Ronneka Newell (Ronnie) or Alicia Luke (LeLe)

♪ Eight Wheelin' from Grand Rapids

♪ Flint Roller Skating Association, my man Kevin Edmonds

♪ Flint Angels, JB Cousins

♪ Grand Rapids

♪ The Knight Riders, Joann Haywood and Keisha Jamison

♪ Motown Navigators, Wayne Kendrix, Charlotte Beachem

♪ Roll Call Skate Productions, Lisa McFadden

♪ Sensational Skaters Inc. Keep up the work, Joe Carter; you're making us very proud

♪ West Michigan Rapid Rollers, George Davis

♪ Sk8 Dynasty, Tariya Gunter

♪ Deez Skaters, Kenny "Moodyman" Dixon Jr.

And there are more groups being put together every year.

To the over five thousand skating groups all over the country, keep the spirit of what we love to do alive. Tasha Klusman of Our Family Skate Association (National Roller-Skating Museum), we love everything that you are doing in the name of skating and will help you in any way we can to keep our love of skating rolling for years to come.

The best parts about going skating are meeting so many nice people, the exercise you get from moving all the parts of your body, and all the new steps you learn. When you go skating, your mind is in another zone. When skating is over, then you come back to your normal thinking. Motown's music taught us how to groove with another beat.

Thank you, Mr. Gordy; you're a genius, and your music has inspired me to write *The Motown Sound on Wheels*. When you read this story, I hope you remember when you were at the Arcadia and the vibes you felt from all the skaters who were jammin' to your music.

The Future of Skating Rolls On

I'M GOING TO MAKE A movie honoring what the Arcadia was all about. I want to do several movies about the life and times of some of the best roller skaters in the world, because skaters from all over the world can relate to the Motown Sound. One day we will have a traveling roller-skating show with the best skaters on the globe, just like the ice skaters. Our advantage over ice skaters is that we will be able to roller skate year-round.

There are over five thousand rinks all over the country and over four thousand more in other places around the world to skate in. We can add to that population the Internet, and we've gone global with Skategroove. com, Jivebiscuit.com, and Facebook, with even more websites popping up every year telling us what's going on in the roller-skating world and advertising all the skating parties that are coming up, too. Because of the Internet, we can even talk to skaters on the other side of the world. Things are just getting better for us roller skaters to stay connected, and we've only just begun. We are planning animations and cartoons about the Motown Sound on wheels where skaters will be doing all kinds of things on skates. The future holds a Broadway musical about the Motown Sound on wheels. The production will bring the house down and show the world the extraordinary talents of skaters on wheels on a stage.

We won't stop there, either. We plan to have the biggest roller-skating party in the world. Stars will come from all over the world to jam with us. Rap, jazz, and R&B have taken the Motown Sound and made good music out of it.

Epilogue

I'VE BEEN SKATING FOR DECADES now and I've only shared a portion of
the roller-skating world that I grew up in and the future I see for skaters
everywhere. But there is a new generation of passionate, committed, and
adventurous skaters rising, even as I complete this book. They too have a
story about their love for skating. I will be interviewing them, and there
will be a book two for *The Motown Sound on Wheels*.

In the next book, skaters will talk about their lives and passion
for skating in greater detail. Some of the names of skaters in the next
volume are:

Adelaide (candoitbyherself) Princess
Angela Moore
Anthony (Airbrushtone) Miles
Antonio Vant
Chuck Williams
Clark Dillon
Cynthia Roberts
Erica Hill
Ebony Civilus
Edward Reese
Dave (Be-Rockin) Jones
David Cross
Karen Wiggins

Ken Riley
Marc A. Gantt
Larry Payne
Markita Ridley
Marsha Shelman
Bridgette Robinson
Carlesa Williams
Pat Byrd
Rita (coco) Baker Rivera
Robyn Edwards
Patricia Giles
Theresa Jones
Perry Stokes
Quinton Green
Cyndi Knox
Mildrea Smith
Treanye (got her own)
Richard Stephens
Doe Boy Johnson
Wayne Kendrix
Stephanie (Irideitlikeistoleit) Wade
Shlinda (Funsizeskater)
Tiffany Brown
Rafael Bryant
William D. Williams

The skaters listed above are also the ones who will take the next generation of skaters to an even higher level than ever before. Watch out for their stories. They will make you slide into the corner. They will let non-skaters and the world at large better understand what I mean about *The Motown Sound on Wheels.*

~ROCKIN RICHARD HOUSTON

Rockin' Richard
Houston's Roller
Skating Résumé

Email:
Flomat777@aol.com

PERFORMANCES

- ♪ *Kelly & Company*: ABC, Detroit, Michigan. Two appearances.
- ♪ *PM Magazine*: ABC, Detroit, Michigan
- ♪ *The Gong Show*: NBC, Los Angeles, California. Return Guest Appearance
- ♪ Heublein Company: Performer for Brass Monkey, Hartford, Connecticut
- ♪ Boblo Boat: Detroit, Michigan
- ♪ Thanksgiving Day Parade: Detroit, MI
- ♪ *ABC Afterschool Special*: Los Angeles, California
- ♪ The Detroit Doc's Film Festival: Performer after the film: *8 Wheels and Some Soul Brotha Music*
- ♪ Marla Gibbs's Club: Los Angeles, California, Performer, Second-Place Winner
- ♪ Opening act for James Brown: Detroit, Michigan
- ♪ Freeport, Bahamas: performed for over 3,000 skaters
- ♪ Fashion Model on Skates: Modeling Agencies, Detroit, Michigan

INSTRUCTOR TO NOTABLE CLIENTS:

Bernie Casey
Kareem Abdul-Jabbar

Jim Brown

Cher

John Amos

Plus, over 10,000 Detroit skaters

DETROIT MOVES

Here are the names of some of my own moves and other skating moves
that Detroit skaters would be familiar with:

♪ The Shuffle forward – Rockin' Richard
♪ The Shuffle backward – Rockin' Richard
♪ The Shuffle forward with a drop – Rockin' Richard
♪ The Shuffle backward with a drop – Rockin' Richard
♪ The in and out with a high kick at the end – Rockin' Richard
♪ The in and out with a snap kick at the end – Rockin' Richard
♪ Rockin' Richard's Superman drop
♪ One leg slide left or right – Rockin' Richard
♪ Inside slide with four wheels – Rockin' Richard
♪ Inside slide left foot – Rockin' Richard
♪ Shot the duck with a drop – Rockin' Richard
♪ Reverse turn around
♪ Double reverse turn around
♪ Kenny Mack
♪ Pontiac
♪ Stepping in the middle of the floor
♪ Open house sliding
♪ Sliding into the corner, tapping the left and right foot

CPSIA information can be obtained
at www.ICGtesting.com
Printed in the USA
BVHW050600120421
604724BV00003B/662

9 781535 614016